modern fatigue

modern fatigue

you can recover and stay recovered

Sue Besomo

LAMPINI
Gold Coast

Copyright © 2025 by Sue Besomo

All rights reserved. No part of this publication may be reproduced by any mechanical, photographic or electronic process, or in the form of a phonographic recording, nor may it be stored in a retrieval system, transmitted or otherwise be copied for public or private use - other than for fair use as brief quotations embodied in articles and reviews - without prior written permission of the publisher.

This book contains information relating to healthcare. It should be used to supplement rather than replace the advice of your doctor or another trained healthcare professional. If you know or suspect you have a health problem, it is recommended that you seek your physician's advice before embarking on any health or medical program or treatment. All efforts have been made to ensure the accuracy of the information contained in this book as of the date of publication. The publisher and the author disclaim liability for any outcomes that may occur as a result of applying the methods suggested in this book.

Published in Australia in 2025 by Lampini Publishing
PO Box 111, Miami, Queensland 4220

Cover design by Peter Long
Interior design by Peter Long
Author photograph by Kate Smith

A catalogue record for this book is available from the National Library of Australia

ISBN 978-1-7637426-0-4
e-book ISBN 978-1-7637426-2-8

The author Sue Besomo declares that she has no financial affiliations with any organisations or individuals mentioned in this book, and that no AI was used in writing this book.

Contents

Introduction 1
    My Story 1
    This Book 3

Energy Thief #1: Blurred Personal Boundaries 7
    My Story continued... 7
    How blurred boundaries steal our energy 9
    Developing strong boundaries 11
    Toolkit for arresting Energy Thief #1 14

Energy Thief #2: Lack of Meaning 17
    My Story continued... 17
    How lack of meaning steals our energy 19
    Finding meaning 20
    Toolkit for arresting Energy Thief #2 24

Energy Thief #3: Imbalance 27
    My Story continued... 27
    How imbalance steals our energy 29
    Achieving balance 30
    Toolkit for arresting Energy Thief #3 35

Energy Thief #4: Mistaken Personal Narratives 37
    My Story continued... 37
    How mistaken personal narratives steal our energy 40
    Changing the default mode network 40
    Toolkit for arresting Energy Thief #4 45

Energy Thief #5: Emotional Overload 47
    My Story continued... 47
    How emotional overload steals our energy 49
    Protecting ourselves from absorbing other people's pain 51
    Integrating our own strong emotions 52
    Completing the stress cycle 54
    Toolkit for arresting Energy Thief #5 55

Energy Thief #6: Our Burnout Society 57
    My Story continued... 57
    How our burnout society steals our energy 59
    Developing the mindset of hardiness 61
    Toolkit for arresting Energy Thief #6 65

Energy Thief #7: Low Fuel Reserves 67
    My Story continued... 67
    How low fuel reserves steal our energy 69
    Causes of insulin resistance 71
    Ensuring adequate fuel reserves 72
    Toolkit for arresting Energy Thief #7 75

Energy Thief #8: Chronic Inflammation 77
    My Story continued... 78
    How chronic inflammation steals our energy 79
    General causes of chronic inflammation 80
    Steps towards reducing chronic inflammation 84
    Toolkit for arresting Energy Thief #8 86

Energy Thief #9: Disordered Breathing 89
    My Story continued… 89
    How disordered breathing steals our energy 91
    Regulating the breath 92
    A word about hydration 94
    Achieving a healthy fluid balance 95
    Toolkit for arresting Energy Thief #9 97

Epilogue 99
    My Story summed up 100
    Your personal plan 101

Acknowledgements 103
About the Author 105
Notes 107

Introduction

From my own lengthy experience of modern fatigue, I know how it can affect almost every area of life. I also now know that it is not something that we simply have to put up with. I recovered *and so can you.*

My Story

When I was at the height of my nursing career I burnt myself out to the point where I had to resign from work to recover. Fatigue and brain fog made it impossible for me to function effectively as the head of a hospital department.

My GP did some tests and declared that I did not have an identifiable disease and suggested that I try an integrative medical clinic. Integrative medicine combines Western medicine with Eastern approaches as well as complementary therapies. When I asked the physician at this clinic how long it would take for me to recover, he replied, "About as long as it took for you to get into this state." I tried not to think about how long that took - it was at least 10 years.

After more than a year of rest, during which time I did recover some energy, I was able to work again. The problem was that I had to keep leaving jobs after only a short time because the fatigue kept returning. I attended specialist clinics and underwent further tests to find out why I could not sustain my energy. The tests were again negative for any disease, indicating no clear reason for my recurring fatigue. Treatment was pretty much limited to rest and dietary changes.

As I lay on my bed one morning, *15 years* into this recurring fatigue, I listened enviously to those in the outside world briskly starting their day. I wanted to briskly start my day too, but autonomy goes out the window when your life energy falters. I seemed to be facing a rather bleak future where I would never have enough energy to live a normal life again.

While rest and the complementary therapies I tried were fairly effective in the short term, frustratingly the fatigue kept coming back. The prospect of living with this

INTRODUCTION

indefinitely was so alarming that I decided to search for answers myself. I figured that with two research degrees in the field of health I should be able to find out what was really going on. After 5 years of reviewing a large body of research and testing relevant findings on myself, I worked out at last what had been missing for me.

The answers I found came in part from research that had been conducted in two unexpected areas: *unlocking the broader mystery of health*, and *achieving spontaneous remission from terminal illness*. The findings from research into these areas, along with findings from recent research into fatigue, form the basis of this book.

This Book

Modern fatigue occurs when too much of our life energy is consumed by our physical, mental and emotional responses to contemporary life. Having learned how to regain and sustain this energy, I have written this book so that you can have this information too.

When we get our life energy back our daily life no longer drains us. Connecting with family, friends and colleagues becomes a pleasure again instead of yet

3

another exhausting social occasion. We can wake up in the morning without brain fog and tiredness, ready to give ourselves fully to our work and our interests instead of just *wishing* we could do so. Life opens up for us!

Much has been learnt about fatigue from targeted research into burnout and chronic fatigue states. *Broader research findings however enable a more holistic, comprehensive and individualised approach to recovery and/ or prevention. That is what this book offers.* As a health researcher and medical educator I have been able to sift through an extensive body of research and condense the essentials into this book.

The chapters are organised around nine **Energy Thieves.**

These are not human Energy Thieves, but *factors* that drain our energy - mental, emotional, physical and social. In each chapter I relate My Story of how and why I succumbed to each Energy Thief over the years. This is followed by a short overview of the Energy Thief in question, how it steals your energy - and how you can arrest it.

Each chapter concludes with a Toolkit listing the evidence-based recovery/prevention actions mentioned in that chapter. You can select from this Toolkit the actions that will address your own unique situation. There are no questionnaires, worksheets or exercises to complete to create your own recovery/prevention plan. All you need is a notebook and a pen. If you are at risk of fatigue due to *burnout*, or you are already burnt out, the same strategies apply.

Some pathologies such as blood disorders, hormonal imbalances and other disease states *can* cause fatigue, so it is important to see your doctor to exclude any known medical causes.

By the time you finish this book you will have a clear, achievable, personalised plan that will help you rebuild your energy and keep it. Your individual circumstances, whatever they might be, will determine the right recovery/prevention plan for *you*.

Let's get started!

Energy Thief #1: Blurred Personal Boundaries

If the only thing you take from this book is an understanding of the impact that clear self-definition - expressed in strong personal boundaries - has on your life energy, you will have grasped one of the most effective ways to retrieve and conserve that energy.

• • ❋ • •

My Story continued...

By the time I was a young adult I had learned little about personal boundaries and therefore had little self-definition. Our boundaries define who we are and where we are going. For a long time I really didn't know who

I was or what my purpose was beyond bare surviving.

My primary focus being on the external world would see me habitually attending to others' needs before my own. While this enabled me to do well in my nursing career, it was a dysfunctional state that left me under-focused on my inner life - on the thoughts and feelings inside of me. I didn't truly realise that I *had* an inner life until I attended a healing retreat where reflecting on my life path was part of the retreat process. This mostly silent, individually guided retreat assisted me to grieve losses and release suppressed emotions within a supported spiritual context.[1] I also learned that I had to stand in my own power in order to protect my boundaries. That sounded like a good idea, but for me it raised two questions: what *is* my power, and how do I *stand* in it?

Personal power comes from having a clear sense of what we believe, feel and value about life. *Standing in this power* requires us to know how we are feeling in different circumstances so that we can identify when we are stressed and do something about it. Reflecting on my thoughts and experiences was a necessary first step to begin this important process.

One of the things that I knew exhausted me was listening to compulsive talkers. The next time I found myself listening to one, I identified that I was feeling tense and annoyed because I was allowing myself to sit through this. So gathering my courage, I politely interrupted the relentless stream of words by announcing that I needed to be somewhere else. This really did feel right. Like I was standing in my own power!

Knowing how I was feeling both physically (tense) and emotionally (annoyed) in that situation alerted me to my need to create a boundary that protected me from what I didn't want to experience. In that way it contributed to my self-definition. It also created some much needed space for me to get on with doing what I truly valued… once I figured out precisely what that was.

How blurred boundaries steal our energy

Ideally we develop in stages from complete dependence on others as a baby to self-regulation as an adult. As we grow, if we do not learn how to effectively distinguish self from others we will have weak personal boundaries. This lack of a clear differentiation between self and others eventually results in feelings of powerlessness as we assign most of our decision-making to those around us. More or less disempowered, we are not fully in charge of our own direction in life. The ongoing tension between how we are actually living and how we would prefer to live drains our energy.

Boundaries are rather like lines in the sand: they tell others what we do and don't want to experience in life. Strong clear boundaries enable us to conserve energy by knowing when to say no to others' requests. People with weak or blurred boundaries have difficulty saying no to the pressures, demands and preferences of others. In the short term we may have avoided relationship conflict by saying yes, but the psychic energy we build up inside wears us out.

Are *you* in charge of your own existence, or do you allow others to structure and determine your life in ways that suit them? Importantly, it needs to be noted that blurred or weak boundaries *can* have their origin in past trauma, for instance from childhood or from military service.[2,3]

Living outside the truth of our boundaries is exhausting. We end up living scattered or chaotic lives, and living in chaos takes energy. If we don't protect our boundaries we may also find ourselves vulnerable to parasitic relationships, exploitation, codependency,[4] or illness.[5]

Canadian medical doctor and trauma expert Gabor Maté notes that when we are not clear about where we end and others begin, psychological confusion results. This can have implications at the physical level to the extent that the immune system becomes confused and dysfunctional. Rather than fighting cells that are foreign to the body, the disrupted immune system starts to fight healthy cells instead, with adverse health consequences such as autoimmunity, allergies, or poor immune defence.[6] Maté concludes that "disease itself is a boundary question."[7]

Having blurred personal boundaries, or practically none at all, drains the energy that is normally available to us for activities of daily living. Instead this energy gets redirected as a priority to the struggling immune system. Over time this leaves the energy-depleted individual feeling fatigued, unable to properly get on with their life.

Developing strong boundaries

The first step in developing strong boundaries is to examine the *values* that matter to us. Our modern society favours technical/numerical values such as accuracy, speed, efficiency, economy and the like which can distract us from what is truly meaningful for us personally. We can start to identify our values by examining our inner world, especially our deepest feelings:

What do we value in a close personal relationship?
What do we value as personally meaningful?
What do we value in a workplace?

Your answers to these questions will indicate your values.[8] How you are actually living needs to be in tune with these values so as to avoid the internal psychological conflict and external disorder that will otherwise steal your energy. Identifying your values, refining and integrating them, can take time, so this should be seen as a work in progress - not forgetting that a person's values may indeed change as they move along their life path.

We may hold many values that guide our actions, but *core* values are the ones that are *non-negotiable* for us and must be protected at all costs. It is practicable to usually have just four or five core values. Some examples of core values are faith, family, honesty, goodness, kindness, integrity, non-violence, tolerance, balance, beauty, connection, courage, simplicity, creativity, and justice.

Knowing what we do and don't want to experience in life also helps us to establish strong personal boundaries.

A strong boundary enables us to *own* who we are and to distinguish ourself from others. Being able to say "I don't want to do that" indicates strength, integrity, and character. When we can say no, we are making it clear to others that our existence is separate from theirs and that we know where we stand in life.[9] Unambiguous personal boundaries arise from the conviction that you have what it takes to direct your own life. By contrast, reliance on externals and needing to please others suggest that one still has a way to go towards achieving the important life goal of full maturity and independence.[10]

Boundaries protect our values, allowing us to conserve the energy that would otherwise leak away when we betray those values. Possessing the knowledge as to which values are to guide and shape the expenditure of our life energy shows us where to draw the line. For example, if a core value is honesty, then we will choose to speak our truth rather than resorting to indirect, roundabout communication to get our needs met. Taking an approach that respects our core values allows our life energy to flow rather than falter.

Toolkit for arresting Energy Thief #1

START YOUR PERSONALISED PLAN

1. Consider these **risk factors for having blurred personal boundaries** that may apply to you:
   - childhood or military trauma
   - having ill-defined values and feelings
   - feelings of neediness
   - guilt messages from others
   - insistent pressure to conform
   - the presence of domineering or controlling people in your life
   - difficulty saying no

2. Select from these **ways to strengthen personal boundaries** the ones that you personally need at this stage. Write them into a notebook.
   - Identify your core values - the ones that you are unwilling to compromise.

- Attend to emotional pain deriving from childhood or military service.

- Decide the things you do and don't want to experience that are in accord with your values.

- Ask yourself where you are saying yes and where you need to say no.

- Identify the pressures you experience to say yes when really you should be saying no.

- Keep track of your feelings in everyday situations.

Energy Thief #2: Lack of Meaning

When we live without *personal* meaning in our lives, our strength, vitality and health suffer.

My Story continued...

As I rushed around, seeking to become what society prescribed, I was at the same time vaguely aware of an inner emptiness - a vacuum. Essentially I was disconnected from myself and from what truly mattered to me. By not taking the time to listen to my inner voice, values that were inconsistent with my deep personal truth came to occupy this vacuum.

There had to be another way. I had to find meaning in my life so that I could live beyond these superficial survivalist values:

> *Finding and recognising meaning in our lives releases a nearly inexhaustible source of energy for our use....If you do not have the courage to listen to your inner self you will inadvertently live a life in which you have to rely on others' interpretation of things.*[1]

Reading these words in a book on Hippocratic medicine allowed me to see that I had unthinkingly taken my meaning in life mainly from ideas provided by others, often strong-minded or overbearing people, as well as from authority figures and large organisations I had worked for. Needing to live primarily by my own truth - whatever that turned out to be - I began to search for my own personal meaning in life.

The first thing I had to do was to change my default mode of thinking so that mere survival no longer dominated my mind (more about the default mode network under Energy Thief #4). Next I had to consider what really mattered to me in life, to identify what I valued at a deeper level, trusting that in doing so I wouldn't always feel tired and out of balance, aware that something wasn't right.

The problem was that I was living *incoherently*. By ignoring my inner life in favour of external influences pressuring me to conform, my life simply didn't make sense. I was trying to push myself into a standard shape that was incompatible with what I really wanted, with what I thought, felt and valued deep down.

How lack of meaning steals our energy

The sense of emptiness that accompanies a lack of personal meaning drains our energy as we seek to fill the void in our existence. We find various ways of filling this void, many of which are helped along by convenient but superficial offerings from the modern marketplace. In our haste to feel connected to something valuable - a powerful human need - we can miss what really matters to us. This situation inevitably leaves us exhausted because it takes enormous energy to override our inner truths and to live instead as others would prefer that we live.

In contrast, when we find and hold meaning, energy can flow freely to support our health and wholeness.[2] Research on people who survived diagnoses of terminal illness showed that those who were actively involved in a search for *personal* meaning in their own lives had longer survival times than those who looked to an external source for meaning.[3]

Finding meaning

Decades of research have consistently shown that an individual who sees life as holding *personal meaning* for them, has the required energy to sustain their health and wellbeing.[4] When we attend to our inner world and live according to our values and dreams, and when we consciously seek to find meaning within our everyday activities, life starts to make sense emotionally, releasing a flow of energy and improving our health.[5]

How do we go about finding personal meaning?

Pathways to finding meaning can arise in different ways for different people. Viktor Frankl's famous book *Man's Search for Meaning* emphasises the importance of the search itself. He explains that meaning is not static but changes over time and comes through *interaction* with the world, rather than something that is found exclusively in the psyche. These interactions may be everyday activities such as preparing food, gardening, engaging with others, performing tasks at work, or even experiencing unavoidable suffering.[6] In other words, meaning can be found in *any* moment and in how we choose to respond to that moment.

Frankl's message for us is that we all have an innate drive to find meaning. A person who is consciously focused on finding meaning is more likely to participate in activities with a strong spirit and a clear awareness of what they are doing and why they are doing it.[7] This is not necessarily about seeking a final, all-inclusive reason for being (although that is also possible). Rather it is about the seeking of meaning in everyday events and happenings.[8]

Being *mindful* as we interact with the world can also lead us towards finding meaning. Buddhist monk Thich Nhat Hanh teaches us that mindfulness occurs when we are focusing our mind entirely on whatever we are doing as if it is the most important thing in our life. This enables us to take hold of our own consciousness during our various tasks instead of just wandering unconsciously through our days.[9] Quietly observing our responses to events as they happen can show us what we value and need, providing a pathway towards finding our own unique meaning in life.[10,11]

Returning to Viktor Frankl, emerging from his work are certain *principles* that can provide a supporting framework for our search for meaning. These principles include noticing our fearful or negative thinking patterns and knowing that we are free to choose how we respond to events. For example, we can choose whether to rise to a challenge or remain trapped in fearful thinking. Another principle is to understand that there is a force within us that naturally wants and seeks meaningfulness in our existence. This force is so strong in us that if thwarted we may find ourselves subscribing to meaning that is really quite shallow, that does not extend beyond oneself nor contribute in any worthwhile way to the world. Another key principle is to consider what truly matters to us in life.[12]

Research supports Frankl's analysis that there are three pathways to finding meaning: through our work, when we love or are loved, or in overcoming personal adversity.[13] Some of us may use our adverse life experiences to help and inspire others. Some may discover a talent that enables them to add beauty and goodness to the world. Others seek truth through research or study, using the knowledge gained to benefit the community. Your personal meaning or truth may change over time as your self-awareness and circumstances change. The important thing is the decision to find meaning in our experiences.

To reiterate: it is the *decision* to seek meaning that is important.[14] We have it in our nature to impose meaning on events, and if we don't take hold of our own consciousness then what we impose may amount to a revival of past hurts.[15] Meaning in life differs for each of us and can change over time. While each person's path to meaning is unique, the common feature is that meaning in life goes beyond oneself in a way that enriches the world.[16]

Toolkit for arresting Energy Thief #2

CONTINUE YOUR PERSONALISED PLAN

1. Consider these **risk factors for having a lack of meaning** that may apply to you:

    - neglect of your inner world (thoughts, values, beliefs, feelings)
    - denying your personal truth by conforming to avoid emotional discomfort
    - incoherence between your inner world and your outer world
    - strong default survival patterns

2. Select from these **ways to find meaning in your life** those that you personally need at this stage. Write them into your notebook.

    - Pay attention to your inner world; for example, quietly observe your personal responses to everyday events. Your inner world includes your thoughts, feelings, beliefs and values.

- Search for meaning in everyday happenings.
- Consider what matters to you in life.
- Take hold of your consciousness through practicing mindfulness.

Energy Thief #3: Imbalance

Extremes of anything will alter the balance of our human nature. And when balance is lost, fatigue starts to grow. As the body attempts to restore equilibrium, while at the same time working against strong unbalancing forces, it uses up available energy, leaving us feeling depleted.

My Story continued...

The dislocations of shift work and the demands of acute clinical nursing, combined with growing fatigue, caused me to consider a change of direction in my nursing career. In an attempt to make my working life more structured and predictable, I moved into nurse education. The regular hours and pre-planned work program certainly agreed with my need for order. It wasn't long however before I unthinkingly brought my perfectionism to bear on this new role. Perfectionism I now realise is a pathway to stress and exhaustion. Previously I had assumed that the source of stress lay *only* in my external world - in the job itself for example - rather than in my *own* perfectionist attitude.

As my career progressed (between bouts of fatigue) I became known as someone who could 'get things done'. I was always available, willing and able to take on extra work and longer hours, and to be quick to complete urgent projects. Committees were formed and I was on them. My scholarly achievements too were often fuelled by a need to excel, although I really did love academic work and planning educational events.

At home I became the person who could fix everything, help everyone, be everywhere, and manage all the crises that can arise from a busy household seemingly in a perpetual state of disorder. I enabled everyone to depend on me to be their caretaker.

Externally focused as I was meant that I hardly recognised what my own needs were. Trying to function under the mistaken belief that I had to be good at everything drove me into chronic stress and increasing fatigue. My life was unbalanced; it was skewed towards performance, attracting positive regard, and fixing everything. No wonder my energy was running low!

How imbalance steals our energy

Extremes of work, exercise, inactivity, stress, food, sleeplessness, anything really, can create imbalance. Take for example over-conscientiousness. Perhaps we believe that we must do things to a very high standard in order to meet others' expectations of us, especially the perceived expectations of parents, teachers, bosses, and other important figures. Or we may feel that we have to earn the acceptance of others. When conscientiousness becomes extreme and unrelenting, we lose our balance.

What is it that drives us to extremes? There can be many contributing factors including the need to avoid chaos, childhood or military trauma,[1,2] extreme competitiveness, or the experience of chronic stress.

Chronic stress pushes us out of balance because we are spending too much time plugged into the stress-inducing, adrenalin-charged sympathetic nervous system, and too little time under the governance of the parasympathetic nervous system whose function is to rebalance us. Simply put, we are too often in fight, flight or freeze mode. In this energy-depleted state the body continues to seek equilibrium to support our life-sustaining metabolism. It does this by drawing on the energy that we would normally use for activities of daily living, creating a deficit that leaves us feeling exhausted.

Achieving balance

William Stewart MD, author of *Deep Medicine*, was once asked by a group of medical students if he could define health in one word. He replied, "Balance." His students then asked him to define healing, to which he answered, "Change!", because change is necessary to rebalance an unbalanced life.[3] Stewart relates that he has learned a great deal about having a life in balance through stacking and balancing river rocks on top of one another. He describes it as a form of meditation that brings him into the present moment.[4]

Stewart isn't the only medical doctor to understand the idea of life balance through the stacking of rocks. In her book *Mind Over Medicine,* Lissa Rankin MD tells how a stack of balanced stones exemplifies for her the balance required for the different areas of human wellness - physical, mental, emotional and spiritual - to work together.[5] Achieving balance requires a conscious effort and a willingness to change. Listed below are evidence-based ways to restore and maintain balance:

- Keeping account of our *energy expenditure* helps us to pace ourselves. Take stock throughout the day of your use of energy and see where it is spent. Are you spending it on trivial concerns? Are you compromising your values in surrendering boundaries?[6] Also notice where you experience an increase in personal energy, so that you know what energises you.[7]

- Striking a balance between our stress-inducing sympathetic response and the rebalancing effect of the parasympathetic state can be achieved through *body awareness* and inducing the relaxation response. Autogenic Training[8] is a program of six simple exercises using the imagery of body heaviness and temperature, along with cardiac and breath regulation. You can learn these 5-minute exercises via a free Vimeo recording.[9]

- A 2018 review of published research studies explored various contemplative activities that regulate breathing to achieve stress reduction. These activities focus on *vagal breathing*: slow diaphragmatic breathing with longer exhalation than inhalation. This breathing pattern replaces the upper chest shallow breathing associated with stress, helping to restore autonomic balance.[10]

- Recognising and appreciating our *underlying connectedness* both to the visible and invisible world ensures that we avoid living a lopsided, externally-driven life. This can be a challenge in a world marked by attention-seeking media, commuter haste, noise saturation, and fast-paced environments.[11]

- Taking *restful breaks* during periods of focused work can balance mental and physical energy.

- *Mindfulness* is a powerful re-balancer as it draws us into equilibrium mentally and physically.

Examples include being mindful of your breath, centering yourself,[12] or giving your attention wholly to what you are doing in the moment so that it becomes the only thing on your mind.

- *Yoga* has been shown to improve both physical balance[13] and mental balance.[14]

- Sleep/wake patterns that comply with *circadian rhythms* (24-hour cycles that are part of the body's internal clock) can bring about a powerful balancing of energy.[15]

- Cell membranes rely heavily on the *overall balance* between dietary omega-3 and omega-6 fats *rather than on set ratios* of these fats one to the other.[16] How does this relate to energy? Maintaining a balance of dietary omega fats is essential for cell membranes to be able to convert nutrients to energy, a process foundational to energy metabolism.[17] Omega-3 fats are present in seafood, and both omega-3 and omega-6 fats are present in flaxseeds, flaxseed oil, walnuts and chia seeds. However we are at risk of tipping the balance in favour of omega-6 fats because they are also present in fast food, as well as food derived from modern farming practices that use grain instead of grass for stock feed.[18]

Restoring and maintaining balance frees up energy that would otherwise be spent in continually trying to bring us *back* into balance.

Toolkit for arresting Energy Thief #3

CONTINUE YOUR PERSONALISED PLAN

1. Consider these **risk factors for imbalance** that may apply to you:

  - extreme competitiveness
  - high expectations of both oneself and others
  - being overly available as a way of seeking positive regard from others
  - heavy workload
  - over-exposure to trauma, our own or others'

2. Select from these **ways to restore balance** the ones that you personally need at this stage. Write them into your notebook.

  - Examine your level of work commitment and take adequate time out when needed.
  - Take account of your energy expenditure - notice if you are spending it on trivial concerns.

- Engage in life-affirming experiences such as identifying the good things in your life.

- Choose leisure activities that contrast with your work activities.

- Work with your own natural circadian rhythms.

- Practice mindfulness, yoga, vagal breathing, and relaxation responses.

- Try Autogenic Training at https://vimeo.com/showcase/9750652.

- Seek an *overall* balance in dietary omega-3 and omega-6 fats, which are essential for energy metabolism.

Energy Thief #4: Mistaken Personal Narratives

The default mode network (DMN) is a specific network of nerve cells in the brain that holds the internal story we have created about our sense of self. It constructs this narrative from our previous perceptions of events and their semantic significance, and is unique to each one of us.[1] Some of us may hold mistaken personal narratives in our DMN.

My Story continued...

I knew I had to change my way of responding to life, particularly in stressful situations, because my default response patterns of fear, tension and excessive reactivity were quite simply exhausting me. These responses arose from mistaken narratives or beliefs about myself that I had formed and utilised during childhood to ensure my survival. Over time these mistaken beliefs became part of the self-defining narrative mapped into my DMN. Once I had reached adulthood however they were no longer needed, and were in fact a major source of dysfunction.

The idea of holding such false beliefs was first presented to me in a workshop I attended in Australia conducted by Danish medical doctor Soren Ventegodt.[2] Challenging my strong capacity for denial, he told me that I needed to identify the false beliefs I was living out of, and then to let them go.

Identifying these beliefs required me to examine the experiences in my life that consistently triggered tension and fear. These experiences often related to interactions with others - interactions that I automatically, and sometimes unconsciously, sensed to be emotionally unsafe for me.

Three mistaken beliefs that I held in my DMN were:

1. **I need to dismiss difficult emotions in order to be able to manage everything.**
   It takes a huge amount of energy to suppress

our emotions, more than it takes to actually process them.

2. **My needs are secondary to the needs of others, and I have to defer to those in authority to feel safe.**
This belief meant that I was not in charge of my own life, the result being inner tension between how I was living and how I really wanted to live.

3. **I have to gain approval in order to survive in this world.**
Gaining approval took the place of acknowledging my own authentic needs, so again I was living as others preferred me to live.

An exhausting state of affairs!

Understanding that I had been living out of this false personal narrative was helpful, but I had to go further. I had to find a way of letting these beliefs go, of deactivating them in order to develop new response patterns that would preserve my energy rather than draining it.

·· ❋ ··

How mistaken personal narratives steal our energy

When our personal narratives hold beliefs about ourselves that are mistaken, for example "I am inferior to others" or "I am unloveable", it produces responses to life that leave us exhausted as we vainly try to override them.[3]

The self-referencing DMN swings into action when we are *mind wandering*, presenting us then with any mistaken beliefs we may hold about ourselves. These beliefs are mostly laid down early in life, as existential solutions to perceived discomfort or danger.[4] In adulthood they give rise instead to ineffective, ill-suited responses to challenging situations.[5,6,7,8] Mistaken narratives about our sense of self have been shown to play an important role in undermining our physical health and overall energy.[9,10,11,12]

Changing the default mode network

Shutting the DMN down completely is not an option because it does have other beneficial and creative functions.[13] What is needed is the exercise of control over its activity when we find ourselves spontaneously mind wandering into mistaken self-defining narratives.

Down-regulating the DMN can be achieved *in the moment* by switching our attention to a specific task. This is because the DMN can only exercise its self-defining dominance when we are not cognitively focused, that is, when we are in a state of mind wandering.

Further, *neuroplasticity* - the ability of the brain to change its own nerve networks - can be stimulated so as to reprogram the specific self-referencing neural pathways in the DMN. There are several ways to do this:

- Programs of *mindfulness* have been shown to strengthen the connection of the DMN to other parts of the brain, parts that have an overall balancing effect on our thinking.[14] (The practice of mindfulness was described under Energy Thieves #2 and #3.)

- In their book *The Myth of Normal*, Canadian medical doctor and trauma expert Gabor Maté, with Daniel Maté, set out a way for us to undo mistaken beliefs about ourselves. They explain that this can be achieved by recognising that these beliefs are *false*, and then locating the *truth* of who we are - a truth found in our values and intentions, passions and talents.[15]

- Harvard psychiatrist Jeff Rediger spent 15 years studying patients who recovered from diagnoses of terminal illness. He wanted to find out what they did to shift into spontaneous remission. Among the common denominators in these people's stories was the healing of their identity.[16]

Healing their *identity*? What did that mean? Rediger observed that those people who survived terminal illness had worked out ways to change the part of their DMN that held mistaken beliefs about themselves. They moved from having the life-denying mindset of a victim to the life-affirming outlook of a person who determines how *they* want to be in the world.[17]

They took responsibility for their own way of being in the world, thereby increasing their available energy which went into strengthening their immune system. Taking responsibility meant using their personal power to make choices about how they really wanted to live, including how they approached their own healing. Their pathways to healing differed in many ways. But achieving the life-affirming outlook of a person who determines how they want to be in the world was common to all of them.[18]

In down-regulating his *own* DMN, Rediger recounts how he found engaging in new experiences such as structured study, travel, physical challenges or learning a new skill, shifted his focus, at the same time alerting him to his ability to solve problems.[19]

There are several approaches that have helped me with my own DMN reprogramming project:

- The first was the Morning and Evening Meditations of Joe Dispenza DC, available via his website.[20] In 1986, Joe healed his own broken spine using meditation and gravitational positioning as he was unwilling to risk the disability that may have resulted from spinal surgery. His audios are professionally produced and offer guided imagery towards one's personal vision of the future.

- Another approach I found very helpful was a 4-day workshop conducted in Australia by Soren Ventegodt MD, mentioned above in My Story. Dr Ventegodt practices Hippocratic Mind-Body medicine. This requires the patient to step into his or her true character rather than staying within an exhausting mindset that focuses on survival.[21] (Dr Ventegodt by the way runs a holistic clinic/organic farm in Sweden where he offers mind-body medicine, as well as free accommodation and meals in return for help with the organic farming.[22])

- Recently too I came across the work of medical researcher Ashok Gupta, who offers a free web-based program called 'The Meaning of Life Experiment'.[23] In this program he teaches us how to take the mind out of a chronic sympathetic state (i.e. fight or flight) and into the rebalancing parasympathetic state. He also sets out a technique for *remapping the brain* in order to discard default negative response patterns. Gupta's program is worth doing whatever stage you are at in your quest to regain your life energy, its holistic approach addressing more than just the remapping of the brain.

In summary, energy-draining response patterns arise from mistaken personal narratives held in one's default mode network. When we take responsibility for letting go of these narratives and for changing how we respond to what life brings, our energy returns and our health improves.

Toolkit for arresting Energy Thief #4

CONTINUE YOUR PERSONALISED PLAN

1. Consider these **risk factors for holding mistaken personal narratives** that may apply to you:

- adverse childhood/adolescent experiences

- traumatic military experiences

2. Select from these **strategies for changing the mistaken personal narratives held in the DMN** those that you personally need at this stage. Write them into your notebook.

- Interrupt your negative DMN activity (mind wandering) by instead focusing on a task.

- Explore professional trauma healing programs.

- Meditate using guided imagery that focuses on changing false self-defining beliefs.

- Use mindfulness practice to regulate your thinking (see under Energy Thieves #2 and #3).

- Keep a journal where you record your thoughts and feelings.

Energy Thief #5: Emotional Overload

Emotional overload occurs when we are holding in too much emotional energy. This extremely sapping Energy Thief can turn up in two ways: when we absorb *other people's* distressing or painful emotions, and when we don't process *our own* strong emotions.

My Story continued...

Earlier I mentioned my move from clinical nursing into nurse education. Another reason I needed to give up clinical nursing was that I did not know how to shield myself from my patients' physical or emotional pain. I experienced nausea in the presence of patients who were vomiting, and when caring for people with asthma I became breathless. In the Emergency Department, sick people, their relatives and friends were understandably often upset, crying, angry, or in a state of panic. By the end of a shift in ED I would feel exhausted and numb from absorbing the emotions of those around me.

Working in a children's hospital affected me even more deeply. I wanted to leave nursing altogether as I did not know how to separate myself from the suffering of sick children. I moved back to adult wards, but lasted only two more years in bedside nursing before I changed my career pathway to nursing education and research.

Similarly, as a young mother, I was totally unprepared for the sheer energy of a crying child and felt distress and tension until the child was settled. Unable to distance myself from the suffering of others whatever the situation, my energy boundaries clearly were not working satisfactorily.

When it came to strong emotions that arose *within me* during stressful situations, my default response was to freeze the feelings and dismiss them so that I could cope with what was happening in the moment. For example if someone was in direct conflict with me, I would feel shaky inside while trying to stand my ground. My feelings of anxiety and growing frustration could have signalled to me that I was stressed, and that taking time out would have been a good idea. Instead I froze those feelings - suppressed them - and kept trying to get my point across.

I was using my life energy to bury my strong emotions, leaving me feeling drained. Added to that, I was taking responsibility for easing others' difficult emotions even though that was really not my job. The effort I put into trying to cope with my own and others' emotions contributed significantly to my recurring fatigue.

How emotional overload steals our energy

As early as 1957, *The Lancet* published a study that found strong emotion itself does not increase energy requirements;[1] rather it is the *avoidance* of experiencing strong emotion that drains our energy.[2] Whether we absorb other people's distressing emotions, or avoid processing our own, the constant effort required to contain them results in exhaustion.

In any kind of helping role, we can expect to find ourselves in the presence of people who are grieving, sick or injured and therefore suffering emotionally. People in pain commonly have strong emotional energy fields that can be absorbed by a sensitive person who is caring for them. In the professional literature this is called *compathy*, and is described as acquiring the physical and/or emotional distress of others.[3] Research findings also show that some individuals are more sensitive to their physical, emotional and social environments than others, and thus are more at risk for emotional overload.[4]

We experience our own strong emotions as a natural response to certain situations in life. Anger is a strong emotion that is protective of our boundaries, but can be deeply unsettling to experience. Other emotions that may arise when we are confronted with injury, illness, betrayal, loss or trauma include shock, anxiety, sadness, horror, frustration, fear, uneasiness, or disgust.

If we repeatedly avoid processing these emotions we are at risk for post-traumatic stress disorder (PTSD) with its associated exhaustion.[5]

Protecting ourselves from absorbing other people's pain

We can protect ourselves from the energy-draining experience of absorbing other people's distress in several ways: by practicing shielding, by deliberate detachment from the sufferer, and by body scanning.

Shielding involves imagining a physical shield between yourself and the sufferer. For example, this may take the form of a wall of light or colour between you and the sufferer.

Deliberate detachment is about mindfully focusing on the present-moment activity you are engaged in as you assist someone. This diminishes the impact of the other person's strong emotions because your attention is on what you are doing, not on what the other person is feeling.[6]

Body scanning is the process of directing our attention to the whole of our body starting from the head and moving all the way down to the feet. As we become consciously aware of tense areas we can relax those particular parts of the body.[7]

It is also helpful to remind ourselves that other people's feelings are not ours, and that it is not our responsibility to free others from difficult or painful emotions. We can achieve a balance between detaching from the person and being supportive of them by recognising that our "role" is different from theirs.[8]

Integrating our own strong emotions

There may be times when we have to put aside our own emotional responses in order to manage an urgent situation - rather like soldiers in the midst of battle, or first responders dealing with an emergency. Should a situation require us to delay attending to our own strong emotions, what we can do is to promise ourselves that we will set aside however long we need to process and integrate our responses at a later time.

Canadian medical doctor and trauma expert Gabor Maté identifies markers of what he calls *emotional competence*. These markers, which set out what is needed to achieve healthy responses to stress, are as follows:

- *knowing* what we are feeling, so that we can identify when we are stressed and do something about it;
- expressing feelings in a *healthy* way rather than acting them out or suppressing them;

- *distinguishing* between unsatisfied needs from the past and genuine present needs.[9]

At first sight these markers may appear to be simple and straightforward. Being mindful of them however requires close attention and a conscious effort. For example, unsatisfied needs from the past can subtly drive our current behaviour as we unknowingly and erroneously adhere to them as present needs.

The process of integrating strong emotions involves allowing them to be a part of us. This can be achieved by *naming* them, and then *reflecting* on the strength of these emotions and where in the body we feel them. Writing down our reflection reinforces this process of integration because it requires us to organise our thoughts about the experience. We can also process our emotional responses through debriefing with loved ones, friends or colleagues. Some people will find music or art helpful in expressing their feelings. The thing to remember is that feelings have no moral component, that they are neither good nor bad. Suppressing them though can leave us exhausted.

Completing the stress cycle

So far we have looked at both protecting ourselves from *others'* pain and processing our *own* strong or difficult emotions. Self-management additionally involves *doing* something so as to dissipate the physical tension that builds up during emotional overload. Physical tension in itself can cause fatigue.

Although we may have dealt with the emotional impact of the stressor, that still leaves the physical aspect of the stress cycle to be completed.[10] Completion involves *releasing* the physical energy that builds up during the stressful event. Physical exercise such as running, dancing, swimming or sports will complete the physical aspect of the stress cycle. Laughter, singing, creative physical expression and conscious breathing are further ways to complete the cycle.[11]

Conscious breathing includes *vagal breathing*: a longer out-breath than in-breath.[12] The in-breath normally readies us to enter the sympathetic stress state (fight or flight), whereas the out-breath stimulates the vagus nerve to return us to a parasympathetic state, being one of balance. By consciously making the out-breath slower and longer, we stimulate a stronger parasympathetic response thereby inducing relaxation and conserving energy.[13]

Toolkit for arresting Energy Thief #5

CONTINUE YOUR PERSONALISED PLAN

1. Consider these **risk factors for emotional overload** that may apply to you:

   - highly sensitive individual
   - frequent exposure to human suffering
   - suppressing difficult emotions
   - unresolved personal grief
   - blurred personal boundaries
   - difficulty identifying emotions

2. Select from these **strategies for strengthening emotional balance** the ones that you personally need at this stage. Write them into your notebook.

   - Apply Gabor Maté's markers of emotional competence by observing your own emotional response patterns and then seeing where you need to change them.

- Employ the techniques of shielding, deliberate detachment, and body scanning.

- Remind yourself that it is not your responsibility to free people from difficult or painful emotions.

- Debrief after intense emotional situations.

- Keep a personal journal where you can name your emotions and reflect on them.

- Use music or art to express your feelings.

- Complete the stress cycle with physical exercise, laughter, singing, or conscious breathing.

Energy Thief #6: Our Burnout Society

Fatigue has been identified as a serious problem arising from the pace, economic pressures, 24/7 extended work schedules, and other features of our intensely competitive modern society.[1] Commenting on our current obsession with extreme over-achievement, German philosopher Byung Chul Han describes it as "a rat race that runs against itself", reducing the self to inner conflict, exhaustion, and emptiness.[2]

My Story continued...

Amid the increasing pace of the working world and my preoccupation with over-achievement, I was indeed running a rat race against myself. Not yet being entirely clear as to my own values, I simply went along with the values of the workplace: performance indicators, market-driven goals, competition, and productivity - a recipe for exhaustion in the absence of clearly articulated personal values.

As I look back on this, I can see that the punishing pace I set for myself in fact served my avoidance of facing the need for change. Had I recognised this at the time it could have paved the way for me to live coherently, in accord with my true values and dreams.

A major bout of fatigue occurred when I was teaching in a repatriation hospital for war veterans. While these patients had various reasons for being hospitalised, the one thing that was common to most of them was what used to be called battle fatigue, now known as post-traumatic stress disorder (PTSD).

I was able to relate to these patients, feeling as I did as though I had been battling an army of unpredictable and swiftly changing pressures that were foreign to my natural way of being. Like many of the veterans, I too felt numb and uncentered. Persevering for as long as I could, the fatigue eventually became too much and I left work. After 12 months, with rest and nutritional supplements, I did recover some energy.

Each time I recovered enough energy to start a new job, I would soon find myself once again working at a fast pace to meet the incessant demand for multitasking and high level output. Projects were mooted and I'd put my hand up! I wanted to be seen as a capable person, almost invariably saying yes to yet more work when I could have, and should have, said no.

The way I was running my life at home was not much better. I responded to one demand after another in a near perpetual state of tension as I tried to keep everything on track and moving. Instead of using my own ability to figure out solutions to problems that arose, I was more inclined to find an expert and throw money at them to solve problems for me.

Not surprisingly, these unsustainable patterns of behaviour did nothing to alleviate my recurring fatigue. Quite the opposite.

How our burnout society steals our energy

Advanced technology gives us easy access to answers. The downside is that it engenders a self that has no shape or character: we end up becoming merely producers and purchasers. And while the ready availability of goods and services may seem like an excellent thing, it also creates a low tolerance for challenging experiences since we can quickly and easily purchase solutions.[3]

Danish medical doctor and researcher Soren Ventegodt describes our current society as generating superficiality, materialism, misuse of power, and false values. In signing up to an agenda of high performance, market share, extreme competitiveness and raised productivity, our true values get smothered, damaging our relationships with ourselves and others.[4]

How readily our burnout society can drain us of energy! Various forces working in concert have been identified as responsible for this insidious effect:

- Superficial values and a materialistic outlook hijack the energy that could otherwise be directed towards living a truly meaningful life.[5] As we rush to have and to become what society prescribes, our energy is drained.

- Seeking fast and easy solutions from outside ourselves produces low resilience levels, a precursor to fatigue.[6] Of course there are times when we *do* need to seek expert opinion, but not as a general rule for every challenge life throws at us.

- Hurrying through life leads to a lack of self-definition and self-mastery, sapping our vitality.[7] As we ignore the mounting drain on our energy reserves and exert ourselves to arrive at some vague and ever-vanishing endpoint, what we are left with is increasing fatigue.

Enmeshed in our burnout society we seem to be on a performance treadmill. Canadian medical doctor and trauma expert Gabor Maté describes our culture as becoming more disordered and anxious.[8] What to do?

We can't change society overnight, but we can develop *hardiness*: a state of being able to overcome pressures, to master difficulties as they present themselves, and to stand firm in our beliefs and decisions. A state where we are confident we can manage our own lives.

Developing the mindset of hardiness

The mindset of hardiness consists of three intersecting patterns of thinking that together are key to resisting and overcoming fatigue. These are patterns that arise from an outlook that views life as *understandable, manageable,* and *meaningful.*

Research findings published in 1979 reported that these three intersecting patterns of thinking were characteristic of people who did not burn out, despite being in the *same* situations and occupations as those who did burn out.[9]

These same three patterns of thinking were identified in subsequent research published in 1987 on unlocking the broader mystery of health. The findings of this later study showed that the people who *resisted* illness saw their lives as understandable, manageable, and meaningful.[10]

More recently, published research findings from 2020 showed that these three patterns of thinking were reported to be common to people who had gone on to *survive* diagnoses of terminal illness.[11] These people changed their patterns of thinking from feeling helpless to that of someone who decides how *they* want to be in the world.[12]

In more detail, the three intersecting patterns of thinking that constitute the mindset of hardiness are:

Viewing life as understandable

This pattern of thinking understands that unpredictability and change are normal in life. It's about holding to the belief that we personally have what it takes to meet challenges in the face of unpredictability and change, to solve problems, and moreover to enjoy the process of finding solutions.

Viewing life as manageable

This is about having a sense of mastery over life, of being aware that we are creative, competent, and reliable. We feel confident and optimistic about managing our own lives, of handling constructively whatever events unfold around us. This confidence signals our sovereignty within.

Viewing life as meaningful

A sense of meaning comes from our *value*s and ought to be at the very centre of our life, in particular our work. Once we apply our values to our everyday life, and trust both our inner and outer resources to manage our problems, our hardiness grows.

Inner resources include creative thinking, and especially *intuition* - our gut feelings. Research defines intuition as an unconscious analytical process that draws on our life experience and learning across decades, even if we have mostly forgotten it.[13] We need to trust our gut feelings, though at times it *can* be difficult to access them in our fast-paced world.

Californian medical doctor Neil Nathan writes, "If you want to develop your intuition, learn to be still inside." [14] When we are externally focussed, our inner direction is unavailable to us. So we need to be still for a moment as we seek out this sometimes elusive internal wisdom. (We know for example how distracting and invasive electronic communications can be; taking regular breaks from our computer and smartphone can help us access that inner stillness.) Nathan explains that intuition is usually accompanied by a feeling of relaxation and ease.[15]

To summarise the mindset of hardiness:

- I understand that change is inevitable in life and I like meeting challenges.

- I know I will be able to manage whatever life brings me.

- My life is meaningful because it reflects my values.

This mindset boosts our immune system and generates energy.[16,17]

Toolkit for arresting Energy Thief #6

CONTINUE YOUR PERSONALISED PLAN

1. Consider these **risk factors arising from our burnout society** that may apply to you:

- inability to tolerate negative experiences
- constant external stimulation
- pressure to perform beyond a healthy pace
- an overall materialistic outlook on things

2. Select from these **ways to build the mindset of hardiness** those that you personally need at this stage. Write them into your notebook.

- See problems as challenges rather than threats.
- Develop a sense of mastery over your own life by making your own decisions and seeking answers from within.
- Have a strong sense of commitment to what you are doing.
- Exit the performance treadmill.

Energy Thief #7: Low Fuel Reserves

A steady supply of fuel is required to power the body, the brain in particular needing a sustained flow of fuel for its enormous energy demands. That fuel is *glucose*. With the brain having first call on available energy, if fuel reserves are very low the body will experience a state of weakness. Should this situation become chronic, fatigue sets in.

My Story continued...

One day I was out shopping when I suddenly experienced weakness, dizziness, urgent hunger, shakiness, and palpitations. Feeling faint, I rushed out of the store I was in knowing I just *had* to eat something quickly or I would pass out. Finding a nearby cafe I immediately downed a fruit smoothie. Within minutes I felt better. Thinking that this was just a case of not eating enough that particular morning, I was alarmed when the same thing happened several more times. Blood tests and my medical history indicated that I had *post-prandial hypoglycaemia*: very low blood glucose occurring shortly after a meal.

Apart from the insulin deficit associated with diabetes, another hormonal disorder can cause hypoglycaemic episodes, namely *chronic stress*. It was chronic stress that was interfering with my glucose metabolism. The stress hormone cortisol was being secreted far too often.

Cortisol acts to provide fast energy for survival in situations of perceived danger. It does this by raising blood glucose. This sounds like a good idea for someone with low blood glucose. But when cortisol overrides the action of insulin too frequently, it stops insulin from carrying out its task of creating fuel stores in the form of glycogen. High levels of cortisol in the blood will always override the action of insulin because it is more urgent to escape danger than to store fuel.

The long term result of this hormonal disorder was that my fuel stores of glycogen were diminished, eventually giving rise to very low blood glucose levels. Reversing this situation, so that I could rebuild my fuel reserves, required me to change the way that I personally responded to stress. As mentioned previously, my default stress responses were characterised by tension, worry, hyper-vigilance and assorted fears, all of which caused an over-secretion of cortisol. These were maladaptive responses to situations that simply didn't warrant the mild panic I often felt.

How low fuel reserves steal our energy

Fuel reserves are created when there is more glucose in the bloodstream than the amount required for immediate bodily activity. Since blood glucose levels that are too high can seriously damage body organs, excess blood glucose gets transformed into a stored form of glucose called *glycogen*. The hormone *insulin* is responsible for this transformation. The body draws on its reserves of glycogen when the level of glucose in the blood drops, notably between meals.

Glycogen is stored in the muscles of the arms and legs and in the liver. If blood glucose levels become low and more energy is required, glycogen is released from storage and converted back into glucose. Whereas muscles use their stored fuel reserves for their own requirements, reserves in the liver are used for fuel requirements throughout the body.[1] The process of creating and storing these fuel reserves is a chemical activity which relies on dietary and hormonal balance.

When the triggers for insulin release become too frequent, the body initiates a diminished response to insulin in an attempt to re-establish balance.[2] A diminished response to insulin is called *insulin resistance*. For example, a diet high in carbohydrates demands more insulin than the body is equipped to provide, resulting in a weakened response to insulin. The concern here is not about being diabetic, it is about the insulin resistance that develops long before diabetes is diagnosed.

With the body resisting the effects of insulin, over time it will demand more and more of this hormone to try and create glycogen fuel stores. This results in high blood levels of insulin that become increasingly less effective. Not only does this diminish our fuel reserves, but long term high insulin levels have other far reaching effects throughout the body. Prolonged insulin resistance is implicated in heart disease, Alzheimer's disease, Parkinson's disease, migraines, poor reproductive health, certain cancers, some skin, bone, joint, kidney and liver disorders, obesity, *and fatigue states*.[3]

Causes of insulin resistance

Other than a high carbohydrate dietary intake, there are a number of reasons why the body may develop resistance to insulin:

- An habitually *high level of cortisol*, deriving from chronic stress responses, overrides the action of insulin so that the body requires more and more insulin to have an effect.[4]

- *Chronic inflammation* produces cytokines which interfere with insulin signalling.[5]

- *Overloaded fat cells* trigger the activation of inflammatory pathways.[6]

- *Insufficient salt intake* triggers a hormone called aldosterone which is hostile to insulin.[7]

- The accumulation in the body of too many *free radicals* (oxygen molecules with unpaired electrons) without sufficient antioxidant defence is called *oxidative stress*. This occurs when polluting substances such as smoke or radiation enter the body. Oxidative stress causes a disruption to insulin signalling.[8]

- High blood and urine levels of *Bisphenol A (BPA)*, a chemical used in the manufacture of plastic containers for food and water, correlates with insulin resistance.[9]

- *Low thyroid hormone secretion* diminishes the effect of insulin.[10]

- *Insufficient exercise* diminishes the capacity of muscles to store glycogen.[11]

- *Excess fat around internal organs* increases inflammation and causes oxidative stress.[12]

Ensuring adequate fuel reserves

To fix the problem of low fuel stores of glycogen we have to regulate our body's insulin production. That means the resistance has to be addressed so that the body becomes *sensitive* to insulin.

Exercise decreases insulin resistance because it uses up the ready fuel in the bloodstream, reducing the demand for insulin. Regular exercise can also reduce some of the other causes of insulin resistance such as inflammation, fat deposits around internal organs, and oxidative stress. Plan your exercise regime with your health care professional to include strength training as well as aerobic exercise.[13]

A diet of *mild calorie restriction* can also diminish insulin resistance. Severe and prolonged low calorie diets however are to be avoided as they can induce cortisol secretion. Cortisol overall lowers fuel stores, induces the muscles to resist the effects of insulin, dampens thyroid activity,[14] and is linked to chronic fatigue states.[15]

As to diet content, *healthy fats* from food such as walnuts, hazelnuts, macadamias and almonds, and oils from coconuts, olives, avocado and flaxseed rather than from processed oils, increase the body's fuel storage ability by enabling the body to burn fat for fuel.[16]

Time-restricted eating patterns have been shown to increase insulin sensitivity. One effective pattern is to limit eating to two meals a day within a set window of time, such as either breakfast and lunch, or lunch and dinner.[17] If your insulin resistance is severe, moving into a time-restricted eating pattern should be gradual and medically supervised as you learn how to distinguish between hunger and true hypoglycaemia.[18]

Toolkit for arresting Energy Thief #7

CONTINUE YOUR PERSONALISED PLAN

1. Consider these **risk factors for low fuel stores** that may apply to you:

- excessive stress coupled with ineffective stress responses
- chronic inflammation
- toxins such as air pollutants and BPAs
- obesity
- high consumption of simple carbohydrates and fructose
- insufficient dietary salt
- oxidative stress
- insufficient exercise

2. Select from the following **strategies for ensuring adequate fuel reserves** those that you personally need at this stage. Write them into your notebook.

- Reduce chronic inflammation (see Energy Thief #8).

- Develop effective personal responses to stress (see Energy Thief #6).

- Engage in a regular exercise plan developed with a health care professional.

- Plan a time-restricted eating pattern with your health care professional.

- Include a moderate amount of rock salt and good fat in your diet along with mild calorie restriction.

- Avoid repeated exposure to air pollutants and BPAs.

Energy Thief #8: Chronic Inflammation

Our body's astonishing defence apparatus - the immune system - identifies and fights invaders such as toxins and infectious microbes. It also carries out repairs to injured body tissues by producing certain types of blood cells that simultaneously create an unfavourable environment for invaders and a favourable environment for tissue healing. Once activated, this inflammatory response of our immune system can complete its lifesaving work within days or even hours, but if not turned off can cause severe cell damage.

My Story continued...

After about a year of coordinating staff development in a country hospital the fatigue and brain fog returned, and I had to leave that job. Thinking that an extended break would fix me, I basically rested for 3 months but without much improvement. I would feel some energy for an hour or so in the mornings, however the remainder of the day typically would be lost to fatigue and brain fog.

The clinic performed some tests that indicated I probably had generalised chronic inflammation. The physician said that this was likely caused by gut dysfunction and chronic stress. I was treated by way of dietary changes and nutritional supplements, along with meditation and rest. Rest? That was easy: I could hardly get out of bed to go to the clinic! Meditation though was not so easy due to my overactive mind. As for the dietary changes, they included the elimination of all grains, simple carbohydrates and dairy products, these foods being pro-inflammatory. A diet high in healthy fats provided an alternative fuel source to simple carbohydrates.

Research into the prevention of Alzheimer's disease

shows that detoxification through fasting for 12 hours overnight and no food consumption for 3 hours prior to sleep decreases chronic inflammation, and has many benefits for brain health. This has relevance to energy production in that the recycling of worn out mitochondria (which produce energy for cells) allows for parts to be re-used to make new cellular constituents. Fasting also benefits the mitochondria that are *not* worn out by strengthening their energy production.[6]

When I introduced fasting into my healing plan (under the guidance of a dietitian) the recovery of my energy got a real move on. Eliminating simple carbohydrates from my diet had already resolved the low blood sugar problem (discussed under Energy Thief #7), so my fasting program was not complicated by low blood sugar levels.

How chronic inflammation steals our energy

When the inflammatory response is not turned off it shifts our body into a state of sustained defence, or chronic inflammation (the causes are discussed below). *Chronic inflammation* can be devastating, leading to impaired immunity, tissue damage, insulin resistance, heart disease, and cancer.[1,2,3] As an Energy Thief, chronic inflammation interferes with the body's energy system by restricting the flow of oxygen and nutrients to the cells,[4] and by using up large amounts of energy due to overactive immune cells.[5] As the normal supply of energy diminishes, the body becomes exhausted.

General causes of chronic inflammation

Chronic infections

These may be dental, intestinal, or general, caused by bacteria, viruses, fungi, mould, or parasites.[7,8]

Sedentary lifestyle

When muscles are not used, they develop inflammation.[9]

Obesity

If fat cells become too large, inflammatory cytokines can build in the blood and turn on inflammation in other parts of the body.[10]

Chronic stress

The increasing amounts of cortisol, norepinephrine and adrenaline caused by chronic stress wreak havoc on our energy metabolism. The cell receptors for these hormones actually become resistant to them, which in turn interferes with the regulation of inflammation. The stress response can also raise blood sugar levels.[11]

High insulin levels

In those with insulin resistance, high levels of insulin activate inflammation.[12]

Toxins

Exposure to environmental toxins and pollutants weakens immunity, opening the door to chronic inflammation.[13]

Excesses of simple carbohydrates/fructose

These sugars are not only implicated in high insulin levels, but are also known to increase inflammation.[14,15]

Non-coeliac gluten sensitivity

There exists in our society a widespread intolerance to gluten due to ongoing bio-engineering of wheat and other crops to repel insects and to stimulate increased fibre content. Gliadin (a protein within gluten) can inflame the gut causing functional damage. Dairy foods can produce molecular mimicry of gliadin because the casein proteins in dairy are very similar to the gliadin proteins in gluten, a process that can also lead to inflammation.[16]

Gut disorders causing chronic inflammation

(i) Leaky gut Absorption of nutrients from broken down food normally occurs through the lining of the gut, allowing nutrients to pass into our bloodstream and fuel us. We can develop holes in the gut lining which are too large to stop foreign molecules such as bacteria and incompletely digested food from entering our system. This condition is termed *leaky gut* and is one of the most common causes of chronic inflammation.[17]

Leaky gut is itself commonly caused by the consumption of insufficiently cooked foods that contain *lectins*. Lectins are plant proteins that repel predators and are contained in the edible seeds of vegetables and fruit and can damage the gut wall if consumed in large amounts.[18] Legumes such as peas, beans and lentils, as well as nightshade vegetables such as potatoes, tomatoes and eggplant, are high in lectins.

Other causes of leaky gut include fructose, alcohol, soft drinks, simple sugars, preservatives in processed food, pesticides, certain medications such as NSAIDS, proton pump inhibitors used to treat reflux, aspirin,[19] and repeated exposure to stress.

(ii) Disruption to the microbiome The other gut dysfunction that can cause chronic inflammation is when gut microbes are out of balance. These microbes are collectively called the *microbiome* which, when balanced, enables our body to break food down into absorbable nutrients to support our energy.

The microbiome can be disrupted by glyphosate (Round-Up weed killer used on food crops), chemicals leaching from plastic food and water containers, heavy metals, pesticides, herbicides, non-stick cookware surfaces, food preservatives,[20] infections, low fibre intake, some hygiene practices,[21] and excesses of antibiotics.

In summary, the Four Horsemen of chronic inflammation are: leaky gut, chronic stress, repeated exposure to environmental chemicals, and excesses of fructose/simple sugars. This quartet is *seriously* implicated in the development of chronic inflammation.

Steps towards reducing chronic inflammation

- Address the cause/s of inflammation in consultation with your health care professional. Employ the stress reduction strategies mentioned under Energy Thieves #4 and #6. Contemplative activities such as Tai Chi, meditation, or yoga are also effective stress busters.

- Avoid exposure to environmental toxins in your immediate environment.

- Minimise food additives (found in processed foods).

- Reduce your body's demand for insulin production by avoiding fructose and other simple sugars, and by exercising which uses up excess glucose in the bloodstream.

- In consultation with your dietitian consider a gluten-free and/or dairy-free diet, as well as time-restricted fasting.

- Heal the gut wall and restore the microbiome.

The Energy Paradox, by California heart surgeon Steven Gundry, has a clear and manageable program for gastro-intestinal healing which includes food lists, recipes, and lifestyle recommendations.[22]

- Regular exercise is very effective in reducing chronic inflammation.[23,24]

Toolkit for arresting Energy Thief #8

CONTINUE YOUR PERSONALISED PLAN

1. Consider these **risk factors for chronic inflammation** that may apply to you:

- insulin resistance
- chronic infections
- chronic stress

excesses of -

- fructose and other refined carbohydrates
- additives in processed foods
- vegetable oils, margarine, saturated fat
- chemicals such as pesticides, fertilisers, weedkillers
- antibiotics/acid blocking drugs/aspirin/NSAIDs
- insufficiently cooked foods high in lectins such as legumes (peas, beans and lentils) and nightshade vegetables (potatoes, tomatoes and eggplant)[25]

- alcohol or smoking
- electromagnetic frequencies
- fluorescent or LED lights

2. Select from these **ways to address and/or prevent chronic inflammation** those that you personally need at this stage. Write them into your notebook.

- Lower your body's demand for insulin through exercising and by avoiding excesses of fruit juices, alcohol, and refined carbohydrates.
- Minimise stress by practicing Tai Chi, meditation, or yoga.
- Avoid where possible environmental toxins and food additives.
- Work with your health care professional for targeted ways to heal the gut.
- Eat anti-inflammatory foods such as olive oil, green leafy vegetables, almonds, walnuts, fatty fish, and all berries.

- Avoid insufficiently cooked foods that are high in lectins.

- Engage in a regular exercise program devised in consultation with a health care professional.

- Try intermittent fasting as guided by a professional dietitian.

Energy Thief #9: Disordered Breathing

Our body needs a continuous supply of oxygen to power its cells. The breath carries oxygen from the air into the lungs where it is taken up by the blood for delivery to body cells. A faulty breathing pattern can interfere with this process, resulting in generalised fatigue.

My Story continued...

Two factors influenced my breathing pattern as I grew up: childhood asthma, and poor posture from hunching my shoulders in an attempt *not* to stick out as the tallest girl in my class at school. This led to limited respiratory muscle expansion and reduced lung capacity. Years of diminished lung function eventually culminated in loss of energy and chronic insomnia, by which time I had forgotten what it was to wake up feeling refreshed.

Seeking a remedy for insomnia, over the years I experimented with pillows and mattresses of various shapes and sizes, with bed clothing, eye pads, ear plugs, temperature control, blue light exclusion glasses, a weighted blanket, white noise, minimising screen work before bed, and at times, in desperation, pills.

Research led me to Patrick McKeown's book *The Breathing Cure*.[1] His simple, free, at-home test revealed that my breathing was clearly disordered, including during sleep. You can find this test on the Oxygen Advantage website.[2] The pattern of my breathing was disordered in that it was a bit too fast, was directed to my upper chest, and I was breathing through my mouth. These habits were probably a result of this type of breathing during childhood asthma, exacerbated by my poor posture.

I have incorporated some of McKeown's suggested breathing exercises into my daily routine, along with using Myotape, a mouth-closing tape to ensure nose breathing while asleep. The result: for the first time in decades I have experienced refreshing sleep and consequently improved energy levels.

How disordered breathing steals our energy

Following the uptake of oxygen from the lungs by the blood, this circulating blood delivers oxygen to the body cells enabling them to perform their vital functions *including energy metabolism*. A faulty breathing pattern can compromise energy metabolism - opening the door to fatigue.

Faulty breathing patterns include:

- *Upper chest breathing with an open mouth* diminishes oxygen uptake and has been linked to many systemic disorders including cardiovascular disease, as well as fatigue.[3]

- *Shallow breathing* decreases the amount of oxygen carried by the breath.

- *Breathing that is too fast* creates inactive space in the lungs.[4]

- Aside from those medical conditions which affect breathing, ineffective breathing patterns can be caused by how we sit or move, poor ergonomics, genetic predispositions, or a sedentary lifestyle.

Regulating the breath

Patrick McKeown trained with Russian medical doctor Konstantin Buteyko to learn the Buteyko set of breathing exercises which help to control the symptoms of asthma. This was so effective for McKeown's own asthma and energy levels that he became dedicated to teaching effective breathing, and not just for asthmatics. *Everyone* can benefit from ordered breathing patterns. Drawing on his training, McKeown further developed the Buteyko method so as to maximise oxygen uptake and delivery to the cells, thereby enabling effective energy metabolism. These breathing exercises incorporate four simple techniques:

- *Nose breathing* achieves up to 20% greater oxygen uptake in the blood as well as increasing the concentration of nitric oxide in the lungs, which further increases oxygenation in the body.[5]

- *Breathing slowly* improves breathing efficiency and oxygenation.[6]

- *Breathing less air* means slightly less than a full breath, which has the result that carbon dioxide builds in the blood, thereby facilitating the transfer of oxygen to the periphery of the body (hands, feet etc).[7]

- *Breathing down deeper not bigger* occurs when we direct the in-breath to the belly. Such diaphragmatic breathing is much better for us than the shallow breaths produced by upper chest respiratory expansion.

To learn McKeown's breathing exercises you can download his free App from the Oxygen Advantage website, or access his free training on YouTube (also accessible from this website). If you wish to read about the science in detail his book covers the topic clearly and comprehensively, including tailored exercises for specific conditions. Of course if you do have an existing condition check with your health care professional before commencing any breathing exercises.

A 2020 review of 14 published research studies on breathing retraining found that a variety of approaches

- such as Buteyko breathing, diaphragmatic breathing, and inspiratory resistance training - all increase oxygen levels whilst reducing the incidence of sleep-disordered breathing. This review also noted that regular practice of activities such as singing and playing wind instruments delivers similar benefits.[8]

A word about hydration

Efficient uptake of oxygen by the blood and delivery of oxygen to the cells also requires a well-hydrated body. The blood is composed of around 50% water, facilitating the delivery of energy to the cells in the form of nutrients and oxygen. Dehydration hampers this delivery and worsens fatigue.

Apart from not drinking enough water, dehydration is fostered by certain aspects of the environment that are part of modern-day life such as fluorescent lights, electromagnetic frequencies, air-conditioning, prolonged sitting, and air travel.[9] Processed food, artificial sweeteners, soft drinks, alcohol and caffeinated drinks such as coffee, teas and cola are also dehydrators.[10] So too are medications such as laxatives, antacids, antihistamines, NSAIDS (such as Ibuprofen), blood pressure medications, and certain diuretics.[11]

Signs of dehydration include fatigue, diminished urinary output, strong thirst, and feeling dizzy or weak. A well-hydrated body should produce urine that is a clear, pale, straw colour.

Achieving a healthy fluid balance

Balancing our hydration improves daily energy levels, in addition to providing us with cognitive and digestive benefits. As well as drinking sufficient water, preferably filtered, we need to ensure that the water we take in is effectively delivered to our cells. Water stored in plant food is already filtered and holds nutrients including minerals. Minerals assist our cells to absorb water and to support the energy functions of the body.

The amount of water we need will vary according to environmental temperature, an individual's weight, exercise, and diet. We generally consume about 20% of our fluid needs each day from food. Plant foods hold around 80 - 98% water by volume.[12]

If you are sitting for prolonged periods, micro-movements such as gently moving your spine, neck or limbs will facilitate cellular uptake of water and the passing of waste from the cells.[13] To maximise hydration during air travel, drink lightly salted water, move regularly, and maintain spinal alignment.[14] Applying aloe vera cream to your skin helps to hold in moisture.[15]

To summarise: our energy levels are dependent upon the effective delivery of the right amount of oxygen to all of the cells in the body. Regulated or ordered breathing and the right balance of fluid in the body can contribute significantly to achieving and maintaining optimal energy levels.

Toolkit for arresting Energy Thief #9

CONTINUE YOUR PERSONALISED PLAN

1. Consider these **risk factors for low oxygen uptake and delivery** that may apply to you:

    - poor posture
    - sedentary lifestyle
    - disordered breathing patterns
    - insufficient water intake
    - dehydrating environments
    - dehydrating food and drink
    - dehydrating medications (diuretics and blood pressure medications, also laxatives, antacids, antihistamines, and NSAIDS such as Ibuprofen)

2. Select from these **ways to maximise oxygen uptake and delivery** those that you personally need at this stage. Write them into your notebook.

- Regular practice of breath control exercises such as Buteyko, diaphragmatic, or vagal breathing will support efficient uptake and delivery of oxygen to the cells.

- Consult with a health care professional if you need exercises to improve your posture.

- Monitor your hydration to ensure that you achieve your daily fluid intake requirement.

- Support circulation by practicing micro-movements of joints, eyes, or stiff places in your body if sitting for prolonged periods.

- During air travel, move, drink lightly salted water, support your spine, and apply aloe vera cream to moisturise exposed areas of your body.

Epilogue

Congratulations! You have examined nine Energy Thieves and selected strategies for arresting those that have been stealing your energy. In doing so you have created a *personalised recovery plan*. Your plan may appear somewhat lengthy, but you will find that many of the strategies are easily slotted into your day - for instance, ordered breathing, emotional shielding, aligning your posture, using micro-movements, and focusing your mind solely on what you are doing.

Putting your plan into action involves deciding where to start, taking into account what is most important and achievable for you right now. You may decide to prioritise certain strategies depending on how serious the relevant risk factors are for you. Or you could concentrate on particular strategies having noted how often they appear in your plan; for example, regular exercise can help arrest quite a few Energy Thieves. Alternatively, as you proceed with your plan you may just use your intuition in deciding what to do next.

My Story summed up

In looking back at my own attempts over the years to regain lost energy, what stands out is that attending to my inner life was something I had neglected. Instead I relied too heavily on external approaches such as diet, supplements and exercise. These *are* important and *do* need our attention, but they don't address the main issue: whether or not we are living coherently. Are we actually living in accord with our non-negotiable values? Do we see the important areas of our lives as understandable, manageable, and meaningful?

To redress the imbalance in my approach I needed not only to consider my bodily self; I also needed to examine what was going on in my *thinking and feeling self*. In this regard the first six Energy Thieves, stealing as they do mostly from our *inner life*, are more difficult to apprehend as they can easily hide from us.

As I grew in awareness of my mistaken ways of living life, and thought more about my spiritual self - about

EPILOGUE

deep truths that needed my attention - I shifted into an approach that was more balanced. Of enormous assistance to me were the published research findings of Maté,[1,2] Frankl,[3] Ventegodt,[4] and Rediger[5] on the broader mystery of health. As I explored the work of these four medical doctors, the links between their research findings and the impact of the mind on the body became evident. All of this resonated so strongly with me that I began to apply their findings to my own life. This was pivotal in helping me to regain and sustain my energy, which is why many relevant aspects of their work are cited in this book.

My Story of course hasn't finished: I go on seeking to live coherently - at the same time never forgetting how easily I succumbed to those nine Energy Thieves.

Your personal plan

You now have a customised plan to regain your energy and prevent burnout. In carrying out your plan, keep in mind that it is a work in progress; it doesn't have to be perfect or completed quickly. *Any* progress you make will have a positive impact on your energy levels. In the long term, the pathway to better health inherent in your plan can also reduce the risk of developing chronic illnesses. So I would say just take things gently, allowing your plan to unfold at a reasonable pace.

In a nutshell, the most powerful energising idea put forward by this book is this: *the more we direct our own life in accordance with our inner truths and our deepest values, the stronger our immune system becomes.*

A strong immune system sustains our health and wellbeing, without needing to draw on the energy that would normally power our daily activities. Regaining and retaining your energy will enable you to make *real* choices about how to live each day. Fatigue will no longer dictate what you can and can't do.

As you continue to put your personal plan into practice, living all the while according to your own non-negotiable values, your life will gain coherence and be much richer for it. My hope for you is that in recovering from modern fatigue, or preventing it, your life will light up, allowing you to add your special something to the world.

Acknowledgements

This book could not have been written without the hundreds of health and medical researchers who published their study findings in professional journals and books, providing the evidence base for the strategies presented here. In particular, I acknowledge the hard work of those whose books were the result of their extensive reviews of the professional literature. The authors of these books are listed in the notes.

Many of my professional colleagues - nurses, doctors, paramedics, dentists, and allied health personnel - as well as teachers, managers and administrators, contributed their experiences of burnout or recurring fatigue to my bank of knowledge. For their unstinted sharing of their experiences, I owe each and every one of them my heartfelt thanks.

I am so very grateful to all of my family. You have been a wonderful cheer squad, encouraging, advising, and giving so generously of your unique skills to make this book come alive. You mean the world to me.

About the Author

Sue Besomo was born in Victoria, and completed registered nurse training at St Vincent's Hospital in Melbourne. She later attended Edith Cowan University in Perth, Western Australia, where she was awarded two nursing research degrees. Sue has worked in acute clinical nursing, community nursing, and hospital staff development. Following her broad experience in the field of nursing, and further study into burnout, compassion fatigue and behavioural science, Sue moved into academic work holding positions at Central Queensland University, Queensland University of Technology, and most recently in the medical school at Bond University, Queensland. While this is her first book, she has also authored a chapter on burnout prevention for orthopaedic surgeons in *Mercer's Textbook of Orthopaedics and Trauma* 10th edition.

Sue lives with her husband in Queensland, Australia.

Notes

Energy Thief #1

1. Bethel Community Inc., "Healing Life's Hurts" *Retreat*, Gold Coast, Australia, 2000.

2. Maria José Chambel et al., "Work-Family Boundary Management Profiles and Well-Being at Work: A Study with Militaries on a Humanitarian Aid Mission," *Military Psychology* ahead of print, (2023): 1–12.

3. Vincent J. Felliti et al., "Relationship of Childhood Abuse and Household Dysfunction to Many of the Leading Causes of Death in Adults: The Adverse Childhood Experiences (ACE) Study,"*American Journal Of Preventive Medicine 14*, no. 4 (1998): 245–258, DOI: 10.1016/S0749-3797(98)00017-8.

4. Lissa Rankin, *Sacred Medicine: A Doctor's Quest to Unravel the Mysteries of Healing* (Boulder, Colorado: Sounds True, 2022), 161.

5. Jeffrey Rediger, *Cured: The Remarkable Science and Stories of Spontaneous Healing and Recovery* (London: Penguin Life, 2020), 307.

6. Gabor Maté, *When The Body Says No: Exploring the Stress-Disease Connection* (London: Ebury Publishing, 2011), 170-186.
7. Maté, *When The Body Says No*, 276.
8. Aaron Antonovsky, *Unraveling The Mystery Of Health: How People Manage Stress And Stay Well* (San Francisco: Jossey-Bass Publishers 1987), 23.
9. Henry Cloud & John Townsend, *Boundaries* (US: Zondervan, 2017, 2nd edit), 36.
10. Cloud and Townsend, *Boundaries*, 44, 45.

Energy Thief #2

1. Soren Ventegodt and Joav Merrick, *Textbook on Evidence-Based Holistic Mind-Body Medicine: Basic Philosophy & Ethics of Traditional Hippocratic Medicine* (Hauppauge: Nova Science, 2012), 51, 86, 87.
2. Soren Ventegodt, Niels Jørgen Andersen, and Joav Merrick, "Quality of Life Philosophy V: Seizing the Meaning of Life and Becoming Well Again," *The Scientific World 3* (2003): 1210, DOI: 10.1100/tsw.2003.105.
3. Jeffrey Rediger, *Cured: The Remarkable Science and Stories of Spontaneous Healing and Recovery* (London: Penguin Life, 2020), 340-341.
4. Maurice B. Mittelmark, Georg F. Bauer, Lenneke Vaandrager, Jürgen M. Pelikan, Sagy Shifra, Monica Eriksson, Bengt Lindström, and Claudia Meier Magistretti, *The Handbook of Salutogenesis* (2nd ed. Cham: Springer Nature, 2022), 55.
5. Trine Flensborg-Madsen, Søren Ventegodt, and Joav Merrick," Sense of Coherence and Physical Health: The

Emotional Sense of Coherence (SOC-E) Was Found to Be the Best-Known Predictor of Physical Health," *The Scientific World* 6 (2006): 2147–2157, 2155. DOI: 10.1100/tsw.2006.344.

6. Viktor Frankl, *Man's Search for Meaning* [Mini book ed.] (Boston: Beacon Press, 2006), 109-113.
7. Aaron Antonovsky, *Unraveling the mystery of health: How people manage stress and stay well* (San Francisco: Jossey-Bass Publishers, 1987), 19-21.
8. Frankl, *Man's Search for Meaning*, 143.
9. Thich Nhat Hanh, *The Miracle of Mindfulness* (UK: Random House, 1987), 2, 6-7.
10. Ventegodt and Andersen, "Quality of Life Philosophy V: Seizing The Meaning", 1213.
11. Deepak Chopra, *Total Meditation* (London: Ebury Publishing, 2020), 246.
12. Alex Pattakos and Elaine Dundon, *Prisoners of Our Thoughts: Viktor Frankl's Principles for Discovering Meaning in Life and Work* third edition, revised and expanded (Oakland: Berrett-Koehler Publishers, Inc., a BK Life book, 2017), 12.
13. Tobias Esch, Foreword to *Embracing Hope: On Freedom, Responsibility, and the Meaning of Life* by Viktor Frankl, (UK Random House, 2024) xvii.
14. Frankl, 120-121.
15. Bessel A. Van der Kolk, *The Body Keeps the Score: Brain, Mind, and Body in the Healing of Trauma* (New York: Viking Books, 2014), 16-17.
16. Frankl, 110.

Energy Thief #3

1. Mary A. Sciaraffa, Paula D. Zeanah, and Charles H. Zeanah," Understanding and Promoting Resilience in the Context of Adverse Childhood Experiences," *Early Childhood Education Journal* 46, no. 3 (2018): 343–353.
2. Stephen Rose, Alice Aiken, and Mary Ann McColl," A Scoping Review of Psychological Interventions for PTSD in Military Personnel and Veterans," *Military Behavioral Health* 2, no. 3 (2014): 264–282, 264.
3. William Stewart, *Deep Medicine* (CA: New Harbinger Publications, 2009), 18-19.
4. Stewart, *Deep Medicine*, 166-7.
5. Lissa Rankin, *Mind Over Medicine: Scientific Proof That You Can Heal Yourself* (USA: Hay House Inc., 2nd edit, 2020), 86-7.
6. Soren Ventegodt, Niels Jørgen Andersen and Joav Merrick, "Quality of Life Philosophy V: Seizing the Meaning of Life and Becoming Well Again," *The Scientific World* 3 (2003): 1215.
7. David Fessell and Cary Cherniss, "Coronavirus Disease 2019 (COVID-19) and Beyond: Micropractices for Burnout Prevention and Emotional Wellness," *Journal of the American College of Radiology* 17, no. 6 (2020): 746–748.
8. Gaylin Tudhope and Ros Draper, *Achieving Equilibrium: A Simple Way to Balance Body and Mind* (London: Aeon Books Ltd, 2023) 11-13.
9. Gaylin Tudhope "Autogenics Training with Gaylin Tudhope: A guide through the Autogenics Exercises with Gaylin Tudhope," Vimeo recording, accessed 26 October 2023, https://vimeo.com/showcase/9750652

10. RJS Gerritsen and GPH Band, "Breath of life: The respiratory vagal stimulation model of contemplative activity," *Frontiers in Human Neuroscience*, 12, (2018): 397.
11. Stewart, 164.
12. Fessel and Cherniss, "Coronavirus Disease 2019 and Beyond:", 746.
13. Stephanie A. Sontag, Lyric D. Richardson, Alex A. Olmos, Sunggun Jeon, and Michael A. Trevino," Yoga Improves Movement, Balance, And Upper Body Muscular Endurance In Healthy Adults: 2549," *Medicine and science in sports and exercise* 55, no. 9S (2023): 842.
14. Hannah Capon, Melissa O'Shea, and Shane McIver, "Yoga and Mental Health: A Synthesis of Qualitative Findings," *Complementary therapies in clinical practice* 37 (2019): 122–132, 128.
15. Gilles Vandewalle," Circadian, Sleep-Wake Dependent or Both? A Preface to the Special Issue 'Circadian Rhythm and Sleep-Wake Dependent Regulation of Behavior and Brain Function,'" *Biochemical Pharmacology* 191 (2021): 114535–114535.
16. Anthony John Hulbert, *Omega Balance: Nutritional Power for a Happier, Healthier Life* (Baltimore: Johns Hopkins University Press, 2023), 85.
17. Hulbert, 15.
18. Hulbert, 69-72.

Energy Thief #4

1. Vinod Menon, 20" Years of the Default Mode Network: A Review and Synthesis," *Neuron* (Cambridge, Mass.) 111, no. 16 (2023): 2469–2487, 2475, 2477.

2. Soren Ventegodt, Personal communication, 20-21 October, 2016.
3. Jeffrey Rediger, *Cured: The Remarkable Science and Stories of Spontaneous Healing and Recovery* (London: Penguin Life, 2020), 269, 271, 276, 277.
4. Mary A. Sciaraffa, Paula D. Zeanah, and Charles H. Zeanah," Understanding and Promoting Resilience in the Context of Adverse Childhood Experiences," *Early Childhood Education Journal* 46 no.3 (2018): 343-353.
5. Soren Ventegodt, Niels Jørgen Andersen, and Joav Merrick," Quality of Life Philosophy V. Seizing the Meaning of Life and Becoming Well Again," *The Scientific World* 3 (2003): 1211-1213.
6. Rediger, *Cured*, 273-274.
7. Lissa Rankin, *Mind over Medicine - Revised Edition: Scientific Proof That You Can Heal Yourself* (Hay House, 2020), 37-40.
8. Gabor Maté and Daniel Maté, *The Myth of Normal: Trauma, Illness, and Healing in a Toxic Culture* (New York: Penguin Random House 2022), 422-423.
9. Soren Ventegodt, and Joav Merrick. *Textbook on Evidence-Based Holistic Mind-Body Medicine: Basic Philosophy & Ethics of Traditional Hippocratic Medicine* (Hauppauge, Nova Science, 2012), 65-67.
10. Rankin, *Mind over Medicine*, 23-31.
11. Kelly A. Turner, Radical Remission: *Surviving Cancer Against All Odds* (First HarperCollins Paperback Edition, New York: HarperOne, 2015), 258.
12. Daniel G. Amen, *Change Your Brain, Change Your Life: The Breakthrough Program for Conquering Anxiety, Depression, Obsessiveness, Lack of Focus, Anger, and*

Memory Problems (2nd [edition], revised and expanded, New York: Harmony Books, 2015), 110-111.

13. Menon, "20 Years of the Default Mode Network", 2481, 2483.

14. Benno Bremer, Qiong Wu, María Guadalupe, Mora Álvarez, Britta Karen Hölzel, Maximilian Wilhelm, Elena Hell, Ebru Ecem Tavacioglu, Alyssa Torske, and Kathrin Koch," Mindfulness Meditation Increases Default Mode, Salience, and Central Executive Network Connectivity," *Scientific Reports* 12, no. 1 (2022): 13219-13219, 4. https://doi.org/10.1038/s41598-022-17325-6

15. Maté and Maté, Chapter 29, "Seeing is Disbelieving" in *The Myth of Normal*, 422-429.

16. Rediger, 38.

17. Rediger, 275-277.

18. Rediger, 336-7.

19. Rediger, 276.

20. Joe Dispenza, *Morning and Evening Meditations*, performed by Joe Dispenza, music by Barry Goldstein, (Encephalon, Inc. 2017), audio download.

21. Ventegodt, Personal communication, 20-21 October, 2016.

22. Soren Ventegodt, Elsebrane Retreat Centre Sweden, https://qualityoflife.dk/elsebrane-retreat-center-sweden/ (website accessed 3/4/24).

23. Ashok Gupta, *The Meaning of Life Experiment*, performed by Ashok Gupta, music by Philip Fraser, (Dynamic Video Production UK) Film App. (https://www.themeaningoflife.tv/).

Energy Thief #5

1. P.H. Melville and A. G. Mezey," Emotional State and Energy Expenditure," *The Lancet* (British edition) 1, no.7067 (1959): 273–274.

2. Antonia V. Seligowski, Arielle P. Rogers and Holly K. Orcutt," Relations Among Emotion Regulation and DSM-5 Symptom Clusters of PTSD," *Personality and Individual Differences* 92, (2016):107, DOI: 10.1016/j.paid.2015.12.032.

3. Janice Morse and Carl Mitcham, "Compathy: The Contagion of Physical Distress," *Journal of Advanced Nursing* 26, no. 4 (1997): 649, DOI: 10.1046/j.1365-2648.1997.00360.x

4. M. Pluessa, F. Lionettib, E. Aron and A. Aron, "People Differ in Their Sensitivity to the Environment: An Integrated Theory, Measurement and Empirical Evidence,"*Journal of Research in Personality* 104, 104377 (2023): 1, DOI: 10.1016/j.jrp.2023.104377.

5. Seligowski et al, "Relations Among Emotion Regulation," 107.

6. Morse and Mitcham, "Compathy," 653.

7. Thomas M. Skovholt and Michelle Trotter-Mathison, *The Resilient Practitioner: Burnout Prevention and Self-Care Strategies for Counselors, Therapists, Teachers, and Health Professionals* 2nd edition (New York: Routledge, 2011), 209-211.

8. Katherine A. DeCelles and Michel Anteby, "Compassion in the Clink: When and How Human Services Workers Overcome Barriers to Care," *Organization Science* (Providence, R.I.) 31, no. 6, (2020): 1423-4. DOI: 10.1287/orsc.2020.1358.

9. Gabor Maté, *When the Body Says No: Exploring the Stress-Disease Connection* (Hoboken, N.J: J. Wiley, 2011), 38.

10. Emily Nagoski and Amelia Nagoski, *Burnout: Solve Your Stress Cycle* (UK: Random House, 2020), 14-15.

11. Nagoski and Nagoski, *Burnout*, 15-21.

12. RJS Gerritsen and GPH Band, "Breath of life: The respiratory vagal stimulation model of contemplative activity," *Frontiers in Human Neuroscience*, 12, (2018): 397.

13. Valentin Magnon, Frédéric Dutheil, and Guillaume T. Vallet," Benefits from One Session of Deep and Slow Breathing on Vagal Tone and Anxiety in Young and Older Adults," *Scientific Reports* 11, no. 1, (2021): 19267.

Energy Thief #6

1. John A.Caldwell, J. Lynn Caldwell, Lauren A. Thompson and Harris R. Lieberman," Fatigue and Its Management in the Workplace," *Neuroscience and Biobehavioral Reviews* 96, no. C (2019): 272–289.

2. Byung-Chul Han, *The Burnout Society*, translated by Erik Butler (Stanford, CA: Stanford University Press, 2015), 42.

3. Han, *The Burnout Society*, 40-43.

4. Soren Ventegodt, and Joav Merrick, *Textbook on Evidence-Based Holistic Mind-Body Medicine : Basic Philosophy and Ethics of Traditional Hippocratic Medicine* (New York: Nova Biomedical, 2012), 1211, 1222.

5. Ventegodt and Merrick, *Textbook on Evidence-Based Holistic Mind-Body Medicine*, 1210.

6. Han, 42.
7. Henry Cloud & John Townsend, *Boundaries* (US: Zondervan, 2017, 2nd edit), 36.
8. Gabor Maté and Daniel Maté, *The Myth of Normal: Trauma, Illness, and Healing in a Toxic Culture* (New York: Penguin Random House 2022), 363.
9. Suzanne C. Kobasa, "Stressful Life Events, Personality, and Health: An Inquiry into Hardiness," *Journal of Personality and Social Psychology* 37, 1 (1979): 1-11.
10. Aaron Antonovsky, *Unraveling the Mystery of Health : How People Manage Stress and Stay Well* (1st ed. San Francisco: Jossey-Bass, 1987), 16-19.
11. Jeffrey Rediger, *Cured: The Remarkable Science and Stories of Spontaneous Healing and Recovery* (London: Penguin Life, 2020), 294.
12. Rediger, *Cured*, 275-277.
13. Viktor Dörfler and Alina Bas, "Intuition: Scientific, Non-scientific or Unscientific?" in *Handbook of Intuition Research as Practice* ed. Marta Sinclair, (Northampton: Edward Elgar Publishing, 2020), 294-297.
14. Neil Nathan, *Energetic Diagnosis*, (Las Vegas Victory Belt Publishing, 2022), 95.
15. Nathan, *Energetic Diagnosis*, 93.
16. Antonovsky, *Unravelling The Mystery Of Health*, 156-159.
17. Asle M. Sandvik, Paul T. Bartone, Sigurd William Hystad, Terry M. Phillips, Julian F. Thayer, and Bjørn Helge Johnsen," Psychological Hardiness Predicts Neuroimmunological Responses to Stress," *Psychology, health & medicine* 18, no. 6 (2013): 705–713, 709.

Energy Thief #7

1. Jordan Jensen, Per Inge Rustad, Anders Jensen Kolnes, and Yu-Chiang Lai," The Role of Skeletal Muscle Glycogen Breakdown for Regulation of Insulin Sensitivity by Exercise," *Frontiers in Physiology* 2, (2011): 1-2, 112.
2. Jensen et al, "The Role of Skeletal Muscle", 5-6.
3. Benjamin Bikman, *Why We Get Sick: The Hidden Epidemic at the Root of Most Chronic Disease and How to Fight It* (LaVergne: BenBella Books, 2020): 6-11, 63.
4. Yan Yu-Xiang, Huan-Bo Xiao, Si-Si Wang, Jing Zhao, Yan He, Wei Wang, and Jing Dong," Investigation of the Relationship Between Chronic Stress and Insulin Resistance in a Chinese Population," *Journal of Epidemiology* 26, no. 7 (2016): 355–360.
5. Carl de Luca and Jerrold M. Olefsky," Inflammation and Insulin Resistance," FEBS letters 582, no. 1 (2008): 97.
6. Bikman, *Why We Get Sick*, 113-115.
7. Rajesh Garg, Gordon H Williams, Shelley Hurwitz, Nancy J Brown, Paul N Hopkins, and Gail K Adler, "Low-Salt Diet Increases Insulin Resistance in Healthy Subjects," *Metabolism, Clinical and Experimental* 60, no. 7 (2011): 965-967.
8. Kevin Noel Keane, Vinicius Fernandes Cruzat, Rodrigo Carlessi, Paulo Ivo Homem de Bittencourt, and Philip Newsholme. "Molecular Events Linking Oxidative Stress and Inflammation to Insulin Resistance and β-Cell Dysfunction," *Oxidative Medicine and Cellular Longevity* 181643–15 (2015): 128.
9. Madison Wade, Virginia Delawder, Paul Reneau, and Julia M. dos Santos,"The Effect of BPA Exposure on Insulin Resistance and Type 2 Diabetes – The Impact of

Muscle Contraction," *Medical Hypotheses* 140 109675-109675 (2020): 2-3.
10. Bikman, 100-101.
11. Bikman, 179-183.
12. Jennifer Beatriz Silva Morais, Juliana Soares Severo, Jéssica Batista Beserra, Ana Raquel Soares de Oiveira, Kyria Jayanne Clímaco Cruz, Stéfany Rodrigues de Sousa Melo, Ginivaldo Victor Ribeiro do Nascimento, George Fred Soares de Macedo, and Dilina do Nascimento Marreiro," Association Between Cortisol, Insulin Resistance and Zinc in Obesity: a Mini-Review," *Biological Trace Element Research* 191, no. 2 (2019): 324.
13. Bikman, 178-180.
14. Bikman, 143.
15. Bikman, 98-100.
16. Dale E. Bredesen, *The End of Alzheimer's Program: The First Protocol to Enhance Cognition and Reverse Decline at Any Age* (New York: Avery, an imprint of Penguin Random House LLC, 2020), 117-121.
17. Bikman, 146-147.
18. Bredesen, *The End of Alzheimer's Program*, 96-97.

Energy Thief #8

1. Steven R. Gundry, *The Energy Paradox: What to Do When Your Get-up-and-Go Has Got up and Gone* (First edition, NY: Harper Wave, an imprint of HarperCollins Publishers, 2021), 18, 27.
2. Benjamin Bickman, *Why We Get Sick: The Hidden Epidemic at the Root of Most Chronic Disease - and*

How to Fight It (Dallas, TX: BenBella Books, Inc, 2020), 11.

3. Heather Moday, *The Immunotype Breakthrough* (London, Orion Spring, an imprint of The Orion Publishing Group, 2021), 22-23.

4. Gundry, *The Energy Paradox*,156.

5. Rainer H Straub, "The Brain and Immune System Prompt Energy Shortage in Chronic Inflammation and Ageing," *Nature Reviews, Rheumatology* 13, no. 12 (2017): 743–751, 746-7.

6. Dale E. Bredesen, *The End of Alzheimer's Program: The First Protocol to Enhance Cognition and Reverse Decline at Any Age* (New York: Avery, an imprint of Penguin Random House LLC, 2020), 93-94.

7. Bredesen, *The End of Alzheimer's Program*, 20, 38-39.

8. Neil Nathan, *Toxic: Heal Your Body From Mold Toxicity, Lyme disease, Multiple Chemical Sensitivities, and Chronic Environmental Illness* (Las Vegas, Victory Belt Publishing Inc, 2018), 40.

9. Roberto Carlos Burini, Elizabeth Anderson, J. Larry Durstine, and James A. Carson," Inflammation, Physical Activity, and Chronic Disease: An Evolutionary Perspective," *Sports Medicine and Health Science* (2, no. 1, 2020): 1–6 DOI: 10.1016/j.smhs.2020.03.004

10. Bikman, *Why We Get Sick*, 114.

11. Bikman, 98-99.

12. Bikman, 21.

13. Moday, *The Immunotype Breakthrough*, 59-61.

14. Bredesen, 78,79.

15. Bickman,123.

16. Bredesen, 81-82.
17. Gundry, 20-21.
18. Bredesen, 38.
19. Gundry, 42.
20. Gundry, 152, 158.
21. Tomas Hrncir, "Gut Microbiota Dysbiosis: Triggers, Consequences, Diagnostic and Therapeutic Options," *Microorganisms* (Basel 10, no. 3 2022): Article No. 578, 1-2. DOI: 10.3390/microorganisms10030578
22. Gundry, 167-207 (From his website Dr Steven Gundry: print-friendly lectin food lists https://cdn.drgundry.com/wp-content/uploads/2022/05/UnlockTheKetoCodeShoppingList-R1-1.pdf)
23. Natalia Arias Rendón, *Exercise and Diet As Modulators of Cognitive Function Through Gut Microbiota* (1st ed., New York: Nova Science Publishers, Incorporated, 2022), 177-178.
24. Bredesen, 201-202.

Energy Thief #9

1. Patrick McKeown, *The Breathing Cure: Exercises to Develop New Breathing Habits for a Healthier, Happier and Longer Life* (Ireland: Oxyat Books Publishing, 2021).
2. https://oxygenadvantage.com/
3. McKeown, *The Breathing Cure*, 11-12.
4. McKeown, 20.
5. McKeown,105-9.
6. McKeown, 37.

7. McKeown, 12-22.
8. R. Courtney, "Breathing retraining in sleep apnoea: A review of approaches and potential mechanisms," *Sleep Breath*, 24, (2020): 1315–1325.
9. Dana Cohen and Gina Bria, *Quench* (New York, Hachette Book Group Inc, 2018), 2-5.
10. Cohen and Bria, *Quench*, 70.
11. "Oxford Patient Safety Collaborative," Patient Safety Oxford, accessed October 18, 2023, https://www.patientsafetyoxford.org/wp-content/uploads/2018/02/Medicines-that-affect-fluid-balance-in-the-body-draft-SJ-v2.0.pdf.
12. Cohen and Bria, 61-64.
13. Cohen and Bria, 96-100.
14. Cohen and Bria, 18-19.
15. SE Dal'Belo, LR Gasper, and PM Maia Campos, "Moisturising effect of cosmetic formulations containing Aloe vera extract in different concentrations assessed by skin bioengineering techniques," *Skin Res Technol*, 12, 4, Nov (2006): 241-246.

Epilogue

1. Gabor Maté, *When The Body Says No: Exploring the Stress-Disease Connection* (London: Ebury Publishing, 2011).
2. Gabor Maté and Daniel Maté, *The Myth of Normal: Trauma, Illness, and Healing in a Toxic Culture* (New York: Penguin Random House 2022).
3. Viktor Frankl, *Man's Search for Meaning* [Mini book ed.] (Boston: Beacon Press, 2006).

4. Soren Ventegodt and Joav Merrick, *Textbook on Evidence-Based Holistic Mind-Body Medicine: Basic Philosophy & Ethics of Traditional Hippocratic Medicine* (Hauppauge: Nova Science, 2012).
5. Jeffrey Rediger, *Cured:The Remarkable Science and Stories of Spontaneous Healing and Recovery* (London: Penguin Life, 2020).

www.ingramcontent.com/pod-product-compliance
Lightning Source LLC
Chambersburg PA
CBHW060402080526
44583CB00012B/430